EXPLORING THE WORLD

PONCE DE LEÓN

Juan Ponce de León
Searches for the Fountain of Youth

BY ANN HEINRICHS

Content Adviser: Maria Concepcion, M.S.,
Latin American and Caribbean Studies, New York University

Social Science Adviser: Professor Sherry L. Field, Department of Curriculum and Instruction,
College of Education, The University of Texas at Austin

Reading Adviser: Dr. Linda D. Labbo, Department of Reading Education,
College of Education, The University of Georgia

COMPASS POINT BOOKS
MINNEAPOLIS, MINNESOTA

Compass Point Books
3722 West 50th Street, #115
Minneapolis, MN 55410

Visit Compass Point Books on the Internet at *www.compasspointbooks.com* or
e-mail your request to *custserv@compasspointbooks.com*

Photographs ©: Stock Montage, cover, 1, 6, 22, 46–47 (background); North Wind Picture Archives,
back cover (background), 2 (background), 10, 17, 18, 19, 20, 24, 29, 32, 38, 39; Unicorn Stock
Photos/Jean Higgins, 4; Hulton Getty/Archive Photos, 5, 12, 25; Archivo Iconografico, S. A./Corbis, 8;
Photri-Microstock, 9; Giraudon/Art Resource, N.Y., 14, 33; Jeremy Horner/Corbis, 15, 41; Unicorn Stock
Photos/A. Ramey, 16; Hulton-Deutsch Collection/Corbis, 21; Tony Arruza/Corbis, 23; Unicorn Stock
Photos/Andre Jenny, 26; Bettmann/Corbis, 27; Jeff Greenberg/Visuals Unlimited, 30; Peter
Finger/Corbis, 31; Beth Davidow/Visuals Unlimited, 34; Unicorn Stock Photos/Marshall Prescott, 36;
Bob Krist/Corbis, 37; N. Carter/North Wind Picture Archives, 40.

Editors: E. Russell Primm, Emily J. Dolbear, and Melissa McDaniel
Photo Researchers: Svetlana Zhurkina and Jo Miller
Photo Selector: Catherine Neitge
Designer: Design Lab
Cartographer: XNR Productions, Inc.

Library of Congress Cataloging-in-Publication Data
Heinrichs, Ann.
  Ponce de Leon : Juan Ponce de Leon searches for the fountain of youth / by Ann Heinrichs.
  p. cm. — (Exploring the world)
  Includes bibliographical references and index.
  Summary: A biography of the Spanish explorer who first came to the New World with Columbus, went
on to become governor of Puerto Rico, and later came to Florida looking for the Fountain of Youth.
  ISBN 0-7565-0181-4 (hardcover)
  1. Ponce de Leon, Juan, 1460?–1521—Juvenile literature. 2. Explorers—America—Biography—
Juvenile literature. 3. Explorers—Spain—Biography—Juvenile literature. 4. America—Discovery and
exploration—Spanish—Juvenile literature. [1. Ponce de Leon, Juan, 1460?–1521. 2. Explorers. 3.
America—Discovery and exploration—Spanish.] I. Title. II. Series.
  E125.P7 H45 2002
  970.01'6'092—dc21   2001004733

Printed in the United States of America.

Table of Contents

Growing Up in Castile

Juan loved roaming the countryside with his brothers, Pedro and Luis. Their little village of Santervás de Campos sat on a hilltop near a river in Spain. As he watched the river flow by,

A statue of Juan Ponce de León stands in Plaza San Jose in Old San Juan, Puerto Rico.

Juan could imagine its waters rushing on to the sea. But he could never have dreamed that he would one day sail across that sea. There he would explore lands no European had seen before.

Juan Ponce de León was born around 1460. At the time, there was no country of Spain as we know it today. The Kingdom of Castile covered most of what is now Spain, and the Kingdom of Aragon lay to the east. Juan's village had once been in the Kingdom of León, but now it was part of Castile.

Juan must have heard exciting stories about his family's history. The Ponce de León family was not wealthy, but it was **noble**. One of Juan's relatives, Alfonso, had been king of León in the 1100s. The family name dates from that time.

Alfonso, king of León

The Spaniards and the Moors fought many battles.

The Alhambra in Granada, Spain, today

Off to the Americas

Juan drank in the sights and smells on the waterfront in Cádiz, Spain. Seventeen ships were taking on supplies for a grand voyage. There were horses, goats, pigs, casks of wine and water, tools, plows, and crates of food. Most exciting of all, Juan himself would be going on board!

This nineteenth-century woodcut shows Cádiz from the sea.

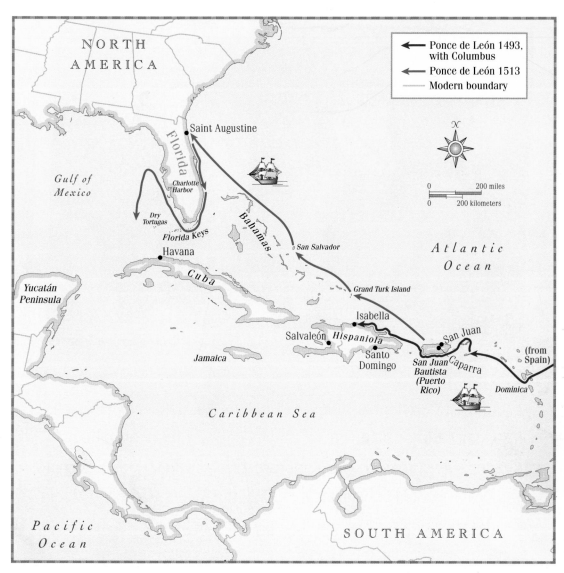

A map of Ponce de León's voyages

King Ferdinand and Queen Isabella

Admiral Christopher Columbus had been in Granada in 1492 for a good reason. For eight years, he had been asking Queen Isabella for a favor. He wanted to sail across the *Mar Oceana*—the "Ocean Sea"—to the Indies. These Asian lands were rich with spices, pearls, and jewels. Columbus believed he could get there by sailing west. But Isabella was busy battling the Moors. Once the Moors gave up, however, she agreed to Columbus's plan.

Isabella needed the riches of the Indies—she had spent a fortune fighting the Moors. But she wanted souls, too. A devoted Catholic, she hoped to convince people in the Indies to accept her religion.

Columbus returned from his voyage of 1492 with amazing news. He hadn't made it to the Indies, but he had found lands that Europeans had never known existed—the Americas. Best of all, these lands had gold! At once, Isabella agreed to a second voyage in 1493. Now everyone wanted to go. More than a thousand men were going, and one of them was Juan.

Along with the others, Juan spent the last night before sailing aboard ship. Sailors said their special prayers for a safe voyage. Family and friends shared their final hugs and tears. On shore, trumpeters, harpists, and pipers played a grand farewell. If Juan had managed to get a wink of sleep that night, it would have been a miracle!

At dawn on September 25, 1493, sailors hauled up the ships' anchors, and a gentle breeze filled the sails. As they sailed off in the crisp morning air, Juan watched his homeland grow smaller and smaller.

At daybreak on Sunday, November 3, the cry arose: *"Land!"* Juan could smell the sweet scent of flowers drifting toward him in the breeze. Overhead, a flock of green parrots circled, making noisy calls. The land was just a small island.

Christopher Columbus sailed for a second time to the Americas in 1493.

Columbus called it *Dominica*, meaning "Sunday." On November 18, they landed on a large island the natives called Boriquén. Columbus named it *San Juan Bautista*, meaning Saint John the Baptist. Young Juan had no idea that he would spend many years of his life there.

Columbus continued on to the island of Hispaniola. (Today this island is home to two countries, Haiti and the Dominican Republic.) He had left about forty people there on his first voyage. When he returned, he found no Europeans. Chief Guacanagari of the local Taino Indians told a terrible tale.

Columbus's men had angered the natives by taking their women and gold. The

Children play in the fountain at the Plaza del Quinto Centenario in San Juan, Puerto Rico. It was dedicated in 1992 to commemorate the 500th anniversary of Columbus's landing in 1493.

A beautiful beach in Haiti today

Europeans became jealous of one another, too. Fights broke out. All the Spaniards were either killed or hiding deep in the forests. Guacanagari himself had been badly wounded trying to protect Columbus's men.

Surely Juan was learning from all he saw. Few Spaniards had the good manners Juan had learned in Castile. And the native people of the Americas could be generous and kind. Historians don't know what became of Juan next. What he did until 1502 is unknown.

Columbus's men and the native people of Hispaniola had fierce fights.

Life in Hispaniola

Nicolás de Ovando was loading thirty ships to sail to the West Indies. By now, it was clear that the region Columbus had explored was not the Indies.

People now called it the West Indies, and they called its native people Indians.

Ovando would be the new governor in Hispaniola. He set

Nicolás de Ovando was the governor of Hispaniola.

sail from Spain on February 13, 1502, and reached Hispaniola's capital city of Santo Domingo on April 15. One of his captains was Juan Ponce de León. Now the well-trained soldier was ready to make a place for himself in the Americas.

The farming and gold-mining industries on Hispaniola needed thousands of laborers. The Spaniards had made the Taino

The Spaniards forced the Indians to work as slaves.

Indians work as slaves. Because the Spaniards had better weapons, the Indians stood no chance of escaping this fate. But many of them fought to the death to defend their freedom.

One day Ovando learned of a Taino **rebellion** in Higuey, the northeastern region of Hispaniola. A Spaniard had set his attack dog on an Indian, killing the man. The Taino had killed several Spaniards in revenge. Ovando sent an officer to put down the rebellion, but the fighting kept on. Finally, in 1504, Ovando sent in Captain Juan Ponce de León.

Under Juan's leadership, Spanish troops from Santo Domingo captured the Taino chief and ended the rebellion. Ovando rewarded Juan by making him governor of Higuey. He also gave him more than 200 acres (81 hectares) of land. Along with the land came

Ponce de León

the right to use Indians as slave laborers.

Juan set up a **plantation** and raised pigs and cattle, as well as sweet pota-toes and other vegetables. One of his most valuable crops was cassava, a root that was dried and ground into flour to make bread. Sailors prized cassava bread because it lasted much longer than wheat bread.

A moth, snake, and caterpillar surround a cassava plant in this nineteenth-century illustration.

In 1505, Juan founded the town of Salvaleón on the edge of his land and built a huge stone

A seventeenth-century illustration of Santo Domingo

house there. By now, Juan had a wife named Leonor. Like Juan, she had been born in Castile. Her father worked as an innkeeper in Santo Domingo. In time, the couple had four children—Juana, Isabel, Maria, and Luis.

Unlike many other Spaniards, Juan believed in treating his Indian workers fairly. He liked the way Governor Ovando ran the island. Indian chiefs were left alone to run their villages as they wished. The chiefs supplied workers for the mines and farms. The workers, however, still had the time and freedom to raise their own crops to feed their own families.

Settling Down in Puerto Rico

On a clear day, if he stood on top of a costal ridge, Juan could see a distant island. It was Boriquén, or San Juan Bautista. Juan had stopped there with Columbus years ago. Today this island is called *Puerto Rico*, meaning "rich port."

The fort of El Morro, started in 1539, perches on the coast of Old San Juan.

Indians working with gold

Indians from Boriquén often canoed across the sea to Higuey, and Juan got to know some of them. One day they showed him some gold. Boriquén had plenty of gold, the Indians told him. Why didn't he come and see for himself?

Juan took some gold back to Santo Domingo to show Ovando.

Ovando told Juan to go ahead and explore the island, but Juan could not set up a town there without permission from Spain. While he waited, Juan lived with his family in Salvaleón and ran his plantation. Queen Isabella had died in 1504, and her husband, Ferdinand, now ruled Castile. He named Juan governor of Puerto Rico. At last Juan would rule an entire island.

Juan landed on Puerto Rico on August 12, 1508. A Taino chief, Agueybana, took him deep into the jungle and showed him two rivers where gold nuggets had been found. He also led Juan to a bay with a good harbor on the island's north coast.

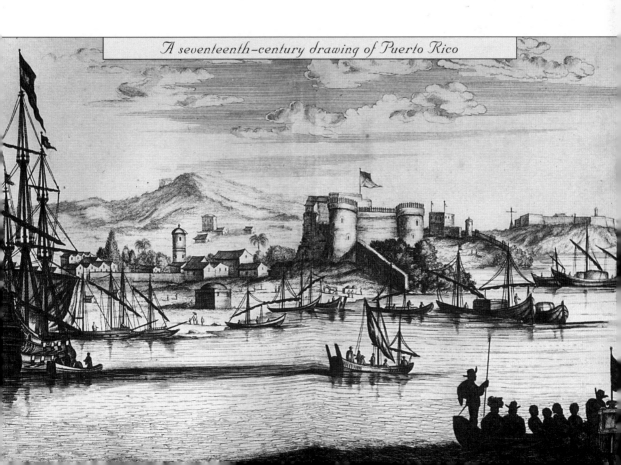

A seventeenth-century drawing of Puerto Rico

Today, Puerto Rico's capital city of San Juan overlooks this bay, which is known as San Juan Bay.

Juan established a town called Caparra. His men built huts, and some brought their families to live there. Juan governed Puerto Rico the same way he had governed Higuey. He started a plantation and raised cassava, sweet potatoes, and

The home of Diego Columbus in Santo Domingo

cattle. He ordered the Indians to begin mining for gold. Juan's family was with him, and things were going along quite nicely— until Diego Columbus came along.

After Christopher Columbus died in 1506, King Ferdinand made Columbus's son, Diego, governor-general of the West Indies. He would replace Juan's old boss, Nicolás de Ovando. Diego Columbus arrived in 1509—and appointed a new governor for Puerto Rico.

A statue of King Ferdinand at the royal chapel in Granada

Juan was outraged. He had worked so hard to get this far, and he was doing a fine job. He was sending plenty of gold back to Spain and keeping peaceful, friendly relations with the Indians. Ovando was angry, too. Back in Spain, he begged King Ferdinand to give Juan his job back. Another old friend also came to Juan's defense. It was Pedro Núñez de Guzmán, the knight Juan had served as a young man.

King Ferdinand himself liked Juan. But Spain's powerful Council of the Indies made many decisions about the Americas. The council wanted to keep Diego Columbus happy. At last they made a final decision: Diego's man would be governor of Puerto Rico. Juan Ponce de León was out of a job.

Exploring Florida

"Juan Ponce de León, finding himself without office . . . determined to do something by which to gain honor and increase his estate," wrote historian Antonio de Herrera. Juan decided to lead an exploration of his own. Everyone knew that more

Exploring the Florida coast

islands lay northwest of Hispaniola. They were called the islands of Bimini. Those "islands" included present-day Florida, but no one then knew that Florida was part of mainland America. The Spaniards had not yet explored that far. King Ferdinand liked Juan and wanted to make up for his loss of Puerto Rico. So he gave him the right to explore the islands of Bimini.

Spaniards in the West Indies had heard a legend about a magical fountain. Whoever bathed in its waters would become young and strong. People called it *Fuente Santa*—the "Fountain of Health," or

The Spaniards thought Florida was an island.

The Ponce de León Inlet lighthouse in Volusia County bears the name of the man who explored the Florida coast in 1513.

Ponce de León and his men exploring the new land they discovered.

"Fountain of Youth." Supposedly, it was on one of the islands of Bimini. This meant it was in the Bahamas or Florida.

King Ferdinand and some members of his court hoped Juan would find the fountain.

But we have little evidence that Juan himself was very interested. Juan just wanted a place he could call his own. However, the Fountain of Youth makes a good story, so the legend lived on.

Juan set sail from Puerto

Rico on March 3, 1513. He spotted land on March 27—Easter Sunday—but he kept on going. He made his first landing on April 2, at a point near present-day St. Augustine, Florida.

Pascua Florida—the "Feast of Flowers"—was the Spanish name for Easter. In honor of the feast, and because of the land's beauty, Juan named the "island" *La Florida*. Juan went ashore to

This sixteenth-century drawing by Flemish illustrator Theodore de Bry depicts the exploration of the Florida coast.

The white sands and clear blue waters of the Dry Tortugas National Park today

lay claim to the land and then continued south down the Florida coast.

At one point, Juan stopped to repair his ships. Natives there told him that their chief had gold. If Juan would only wait a while, he could meet the chief. But Juan sensed a trick— and he was right. Juan and his men took off under attack by arrows.

After another landing, Juan tried to steer his ships southeast. But the water current was so powerful that it pushed them the opposite way. This strong current was the Gulf Stream. It flows out of the Gulf of Mexico, around the tip of Florida, and up the Atlantic coast. Later, sailors learned that they could use the Gulf Stream to power their ships swiftly away from the mainland.

Sailing on, Juan came upon the islands we call the Florida Keys. Rounding the Keys, he headed up Florida's west coast. He reached present-day Charlotte Harbor, near Fort Myers, before turning around to go home.

On the way back, Juan stopped at a group of islands he named *Tortugas*, meaning "tortoises." In a single night, his men caught 170 turtles, 5,000 pelicans and other birds, and 14 seals (possibly manatees, which are large whalelike creatures). Then, catching the swift Gulf Stream, they sailed back to Puerto Rico.

One Last Voyage

On his return to Puerto Rico, Juan found Caparra in ruins. Indians from another island had attacked the town and burned Juan's house. His family had barely escaped. And Diego Columbus was blaming Juan for all the trouble.

In 1514, Juan sailed to Spain to talk to King Ferdinand

A view of San Juan from the harbor today

Casa Blanca, the home of Ponce de León, in Old San Juan today

face-to-face. He wanted to set the record straight and report on his discoveries. Ferdinand welcomed Juan warmly and made him a knight. As an added reward, the king made Juan governor of Bimini and Florida, giving him the right to start a **colony** there.

Juan seemed in no hurry to get to Florida, however. He returned to Puerto Rico and

Ponce de León was wounded in a battle in 1521.

went on with his life. Then he began to hear about outlaws who were raiding Florida for slaves. If Juan was going to start a colony in Florida, it was time to get moving!

Juan loaded two ships with horses, cattle, pigs, sheep, goats, and all kinds of seeds to plant in his new colony. He set sail from Puerto Rico on February 20, 1521. We know very little about this voyage. Juan landed in a bay on the west coast of Florida. The Indians did not welcome the Spanish visitors, and there were frequent battles.

One fierce battle around July 1 was especially bloody.

Many lives were lost on both sides. In the heat of the battle, an arrow struck Juan in the thigh. It was a nasty wound, and he could not go on. His men got him back on board ship, and they hastily sailed away.

They landed in Cuba, the closest Spanish colony. Juan's wound got worse every day, until at last he died. He was buried in Havana, Cuba. In 1559, his body was moved to San José Church in present-day San Juan, Puerto

Ponce de León's men carried him to his ship.

Rico. In the early 1900s, his body was moved to the San Juan Cathedral, where it remains to this day.

French explorers established Florida's first colony in 1564. Spaniards destroyed it the next year and established the city of St. Augustine. That city was the first permanent European settlement in the future United States.

The Spanish built a stone fort, Castillo de San Marcos, in St. Augustine in the 1600s.

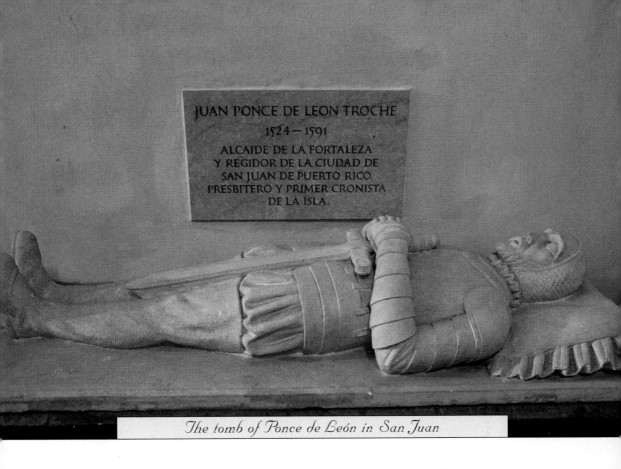

The tomb of Ponce de León in San Juan

Juan's long-time home of Puerto Rico passed from Spain to the United States in 1898. It became a self-ruling U.S. **commonwealth** in 1952.

Like most Spanish explorers, Juan Ponce de León had been trained as a soldier. He could lead and he could fight,

but he much preferred peace. He was a man who enjoyed raising crops and cattle and having his family around him. And he was proud of the good relations he had with the Indians. In an era when cruelty and greed were the rule, Ponce de León remained a man of honor.

Glossary

colony a territory settled by people from another country and controlled by that country

commonwealth a state or nation that rules itself but also maintains ties to a larger nation

estate assets; all the property

noble a member of the ruling class

page a boy in training to become a knight

plantation a large farm

rebellion a fight or struggle against people in charge of something

Did You Know?

❧ As a child, Ponce de León's nickname was "Poor Knight."

❧ Ponce de León was one of the first people to discover the Gulf Stream, a current in the Atlantic Ocean.

❧ Several Spanish explorers after Ponce de León tried unsuccessfully to start colonies in Florida. Finally, in 1565, Pedro Menéndez de Avilés established a colony at St. Augustine.

Important Dates

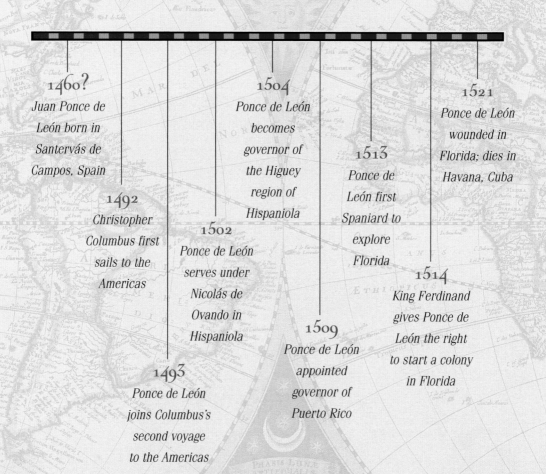

1460?
Juan Ponce de León born in Santervás de Campos, Spain

1492
Christopher Columbus first sails to the Americas

1493
Ponce de León joins Columbus's second voyage to the Americas

1502
Ponce de León serves under Nicolás de Ovando in Hispaniola

1504
Ponce de León becomes governor of the Higuey region of Hispaniola

1509
Ponce de León appointed governor of Puerto Rico

1513
Ponce de León first Spaniard to explore Florida

1514
King Ferdinand gives Ponce de León the right to start a colony in Florida

1521
Ponce de León wounded in Florida; dies in Havana, Cuba

Important People

DIEGO COLUMBUS (1480?–1526) son of Christopher Columbus; governor of Hispaniola

CHRISTOPHER COLUMBUS (1451–1506) the first European explorer to reach the Americas

FERDINAND (1452–1516) king of Aragon, Spain; also king of Castile after marrying Queen Isabella

ISABELLA (1451–1504) queen of Castile, Spain; also queen of Aragon after marrying King Ferdinand

NICOLÁS DE OVANDO (1460?–1518) Spanish governor of Hispaniola

Want to Know More?

At the Library

Crisfield, Deborah. *The Travels of Juan Ponce de León*. Austin, Tex.: Steadwell Books, 2001.

Harmon, Dan. *Juan Ponce de León and the Search for the Fountain of Youth*. Broomall, Penn.: Chelsea House, 2000.

Hurwicz, Claude. *Juan Ponce de León*. New York: PowerKids Press, 2001.

On the Web

Juan Ponce de León: Explorer
http://www.enchantedlearning.com/explorers/page/d/deleon.shtml
For more information about Ponce de León and his explorations

Florida of the Conquistador
http://www.floridahistory.org/floridians/conquis.htm
For the story of several Spanish explorers in Florida, including Ponce de León

Puerto Rico
http://welcome.topuertorico.org
For complete information on the history, land, and culture of Puerto Rico

Through the Mail

Museum of Florida History
500 South Bronough Street
Tallahassee, FL 32399-0250
850/488-1484
For more information about Ponce de León,
as well as Florida's history, people, and cultures

On the Road

Casa Blanca Museum
Calle San Sebastián #1
San Juan, Puerto Rico
787/724-4102
To see the Ponce de León family home,
the Juan Ponce de León Museum, and the Taino
Indian Ethno-Historic Museum

Index

About the Author

Ann Heinrichs grew up in Fort Smith, Arkansas. She began playing the piano at age three and thought she would grow up to be a pianist. Instead, she became a writer. Now she has written more than fifty books for children and young adults. Several of her books have won national awards. Ms. Heinrichs now lives in Chicago, Illinois. She enjoys martial arts and traveling to faraway countries.